REMARKABLE PEOPLE

Tiger Woods

by Judy Wearing

Published by Weigl Publishers Inc.
350 5th Avenue, Suite 3304, PMB 6G
New York, NY 10118-0069

Website: www.weigl.com

Library of Congress Cataloging-in-Publication Data

Riddolls, Tom.
 Tiger Woods / Tom Riddolls and Judy Wearing.
     p. cm. -- (Remarkable people)
 Includes index.
 ISBN 978-1-60596-622-9 (hard cover : alk. paper) -- ISBN 978-1-60596-623-6 (soft
cover : alk. paper)
 1. Woods, Tiger--Juvenile literature. 2. Golfers--United States--Biography--Juvenile
literature. I. Wearing, Judy. II. Title.
 GV964.W66.R53 2010
 796.352092--dc22

                                    2009005152

Printed in China
1 2 3 4 5 6 7 8 9 0 13 12 11 10 09

Editor: Nick Winnick
Design: Terry Paulhus

Photograph Credits
Weigl acknowledges Getty Images as the primary image supplier for this title.
Unless otherwise noted, all images herein were obtained from Getty Images and
its contributors.

Every reasonable effort has been made to trace ownership and to obtain
permission to reprint copyright material. The publishers would be pleased
to have any errors or omissions brought to their attention so that they may
be corrected in subsequent printings.

Contents

Who Is Tiger Woods?

Tiger Woods is one of the world's most successful athletes and the number one golfer in the world. He began playing golf when he was just two years old, and six years later, Tiger won his first Junior World Championship title. In 1996, Tiger began his career as a **professional** golfer. The following year, he became the first African American to win the U.S. Masters **tournament**, setting a record score in the process. At 21 years of age, Tiger was also the youngest to win the Masters. Since then, Tiger has broken many world golf records. Off the golf course, Tiger spends his time practicing his game, working with charities, and promoting his sponsors. Family is also very important to Tiger. Despite his busy schedule, he always finds time to spend with his wife and children.

"What more can you ask for—getting paid for doing what you love."

Tiger Woods

Growing Up

Tiger Woods was born on December 30, 1975, in Cypress, California. Tiger's mom, Kutilda, is from Thailand, and his father, Earl, is from Kansas. Earl was an athlete and a retired lieutenant colonel in the U.S. Army. Later in life, he wrote two books about the game of golf and the experience of raising Tiger. Tiger has two older half brothers, Earl Jr. and Kevin, and a half sister, Royce.

At birth, Tiger was named Eldrick Tont Woods. Earl began to call him Tiger after an old army friend who also had that nickname. Eventually, most people knew Eldrick Tont Woods as Tiger.

From a very young age, Tiger loved the game of golf. Even his favorite movie, a **comedy** called *Caddyshack*, is about golf.

■ Tiger's parents were always supportive of his career.

Get to Know California

BIRD
Valley Quail

FLAG

FLOWER
Golden Poppy

More than 36 million people live in California.

California is home to Mount Whitney, the highest point in the 48 continental states.

Some people believe California is named after the legends of Califia, a mythical Amazon queen. It was said she lived on an island rich with gold and full of strange creatures.

California's nickname is "the golden state."

California became a U.S. state in 1850. Two years earlier, gold had been discovered there, causing a gold rush.

Think about it!

When Tiger is not golfing, he spends a great deal of time on a yacht. Imagine if you lived on a boat. How would it compare to living on land? Make a chart to compare life on land to life at sea. Think about things such as eating, clothing, transportation, sleeping, and games. What would you have to change?

Practice Makes Perfect

Tiger's father, Earl, was a very good golfer. Often, Tiger would watch through a window when his father practiced his swing outside in the yard. He learned to copy his father's movements. It was not long before Tiger was playing the game himself. Tiger received his first golf club in 1978. His father gave it to him. Later that same year, Tiger appeared on *The Mike Douglas Show*, to display his special skills.

Golf came naturally to Tiger. Before he was old enough to play in amateur tournaments, he was already a better golfer than most adults. He appeared in a golf magazine at age five. At the age of eight, he entered the Junior World Golf Champion tournament and competed against boys who were one and two years older than him. He won, and golfers around the world began to take notice of the young **prodigy**.

■ Tiger attended Stanford University, where he played on the golf team.

Tiger won the Junior World Golf Championships a total of six times. Throughout his teens, Tiger continued to win many honors, including the youngest U.S. Junior Amateur Champion. He is the only player to win this title more than once.

In 1994, Tiger became the youngest player to win the U.S. Amateur Championship. This record stood for 14 years, when it was broken by Danny Lee.

The next year, Tiger began to attend Stanford University. There, he studied economics while playing golf on the college team. That year, Tiger was named Stanford's Male Athlete of the Year. After two years of university, Tiger decided to focus on his professional golf career instead.

■ Tiger won his first Masters Tournament in 1997. At 21 years old, he was the tournament's youngest champion.

Key Events

Tiger began competing as a golfer when he was eight years old. He competed in the Optimist International Junior Tournament and won. He went on to win this tournament five more times before he turned 16. Being such a skilled golfer at a young age earned Tiger a great deal of attention. He appeared on television several times to show his abilities. Tiger continued to play and practice. At 15, he became the youngest U.S. Junior Amateur golf champion.

When Tiger was 16, he began to play against professional golfers, even though he was still an amateur golfer. Then, at the age of 21, he decided to make golf his career.

In 1996 and 2000, Tiger was named Sportsman of the Year by *Sports Illustrated* magazine. One of Tiger's most important wins came in June of 1999, when he won the Memorial Tournament. This was the first of a four-year streak of victories, when Tiger won many tournaments and earned the Player of the Year title every year from 1999 to 2002.

■ In 1998, Tiger Woods became a spokesperson for Wheaties cereal. His picture was put on Wheaties cereal boxes.

Thoughts from Tiger

Tiger believes strongly in the importance of being a good **role model**. He says that having a positive effect on another person's life is the responsibility of people who live a public life.

Tiger enjoys helping others learn to golf.

"My dad has always taught me these words: care and share. That's why we put on clinics. The only thing I can do is try to give back. If it works, it works."

Tiger knows the value of practice.

"You can always become better."

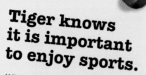

Tiger knows it is important to enjoy sports.

"To this day, my dad has never asked me to go play golf. I ask him. It's the child's desire to play that matters, not the parent's desire to have the child play. Fun. Keep it fun."

Tiger knows he is a good golfer.

"I'm aware if I'm playing at my best I'm tough to beat. And I enjoy that."

Tiger values being a role model.

"If you are given a chance to be a role model, I think you should always take it because you can influence a person's life in a positive light, and that's what I want to do."

Tiger knows that sometimes people make mistakes.

"...sometimes things don't go your way, and that's the way things go."

What Is a Golfer?

Golf is played by hitting a hard ball across a grassy field using clubs. Players start at a tee box, where they hit the ball toward a small hole in the ground on the other side of the field. Players must hit their ball into this hole with as few swings of the club as possible. A complete round of golf has 18 holes. There are sand pits, ponds, and trees on the course where the ball can get stuck or lost. It takes a great deal of practice to complete 18 holes with a low number of swings.

Professional golfers rely on prize money from winning golf tournaments to earn a living. To win a paycheck, a golfer must score below a certain number on the first 36 holes played in a season. Out of 156 professional players in the 2007 tournament season, only 73 received a share of the $7,500,000 in prize money.

■ Golfers, such as Tiger, work hard and play in many tournaments to earn a living.

Golfers 101

Michelle Wie (1989–)

Michelle was born and raised in Hawaii. She began playing golf at the age of four. Michelle was inspired to become a golfer after seeing Tiger play. She had posters of him all over her bedroom. In 2003, Michelle became the youngest person to qualify to compete in a Ladies Professional Golf Association (LPGA) event. She played her first professional tournament when she was 16 years old.

Greg Norman (1955–)

Greg was born in 1955 in Australia. He began to play professionally in 1976. A journalist gave him the nickname "Great White Shark" for his **aggressive** style of play. Greg first began playing golf when he was 15. He won 91 professional tournaments and was the first golfer ever to exceed $10 million in winnings. He now designs golf courses.

Ariya Jutanugarn (1996–)

Born in 1996, Ariya began golfing when she was five years old. In 2006 and 2007, Ariya won the Asia Pacific Junior Golf Championship. Then, just before she turned 12, she became the youngest golfer to play in a Ladies Professional Golf Tournament.

Jack Nicklaus (1940–)

Jack became a golfer at an early age. Beginning at 12 years of age, Jack won five Ohio State Junior golf championships in a row. In 1960, he competed in the U.S. Open as an amateur, placing second. His score in that tournament still stands as the best score ever achieved by an amateur. Two years later, Jack began his professional career with a U.S. Open win. Jack went on to set many records in the world of golf, and has become one of the sport's most successful players. He has written many books about golf and his personal experiences.

The Golf Ball

The outside of a golf ball is made of hard materials. There are usually 330 to 500 **dimples** on the surface. Beneath the white covering is a solid rubber core. This helps the ball bounce. There are many types of golf balls. Some are meant to travel very far, while others are made to travel high in the air. Only certain kinds of balls are allowed in professional tournaments.

Influences

Tiger has said that his father, Earl, was his best friend and greatest role model. Before Earl died of **cancer** in 2006, he and Tiger created the Tiger Woods Learning Center to help deserving youth in the United States. By 2007, the center had helped more than 10 million children across the United States.

Another person who has inspired Tiger is Nelson Mandela. For years, Mandela campaigned for equal **rights** for all people in South Africa. He was put in prison by the government in 1962 and was released in 1990. Only four years after his release, Mandela became the first democratically elected president of South Africa. Mandela continued to promote peace and equality for all people. In 1998, Tiger and his father were invited to dine with Mandela while on a trip to South Africa. They talked about Mandela's experiences, leaving Tiger very impressed.

■ Earl Woods died on May 3, 2006. He and Tiger had a very close relationship.

Jack Nicklaus is a professional golfer who has been competing since the age of 12. Like Tiger, he was a skilled player at an early age. At 22, in 1962, Jack won his first professional championship, the U.S. Open. Jack is believed by many to be one of the best golfers to ever play the game. Tiger was inspired by Jack's skill and hoped to break some of the records he set during his successful career.

THE WOODS FAMILY

Tiger married Swedish model Elin Nordegren in 2004. Elin and Tiger have two children. Sam Alexis Woods was born in 2007, and Charlie Axel Woods was born in 2009. During the 2008 golf season, Tiger had a second surgery on his knee. He had to spend time at home, and away from golf, to heal. He describes it as both a disappointment and a blessing. He was unable to play, but he had a chance to spend more time with his family.

■ Tiger's family often comes to watch him play.

Overcoming Obstacles

The sport of golf has not always been open to everyone. Until 1960, the Professional Golf Association (PGA) did not allow African Americans to become professional golfers. Today, people of all backgrounds are allowed to play this sport. However, Tiger still gets mail from people who think that golf should be a game only for people of European **descent**. Tiger tries not to let this bother him. He prefers to let his skill as a golfer speak for itself.

Tiger is known for his very fast swing. Most golfers swing their clubs through the air at about 90 miles (145 kilometers) per hour. Tiger swings his club at more than 125 miles (201 km) per hour. However, Tiger's swing has been the cause of pain over the years. He has had to put a great deal of energy toward changing his golf swing.

Tiger has never let obstacles stand in his way to winning.

In the 2003 and 2004 competition seasons, Tiger's winning streak began to fade. The way that Tiger had been swinging his club was harming his knees. The pain of playing with an injury was causing him to play more poorly than he had been. Tiger began to practice a new swing. It did not work well at first, but after much practice, he mastered the new movement. Tiger once again became the world's top golfer in March of 2005.

Tiger's knee required another surgery in April 2008. Although he returned to the game two months later, he still experienced pain. Days after winning the U.S. Open, Tiger announced he needed major surgery on his knee. Though he could not play for the rest of the year, Tiger rejoined the PGA Tour early in 2009.

Life in the spotlight has been challenging for Tiger. Tiger's young age and great skill earned him a great deal of attention. When Tiger married Elin Nordegren, stories about Elin began to appear on TV, radio, the Internet, and in newspapers. Tiger has tried very hard to protect his wife and family from gossip and rumors. Tiger named his yacht *Privacy*. He says that his boat is his favorite place to take a break from his demanding career.

■ Tiger owns a similar type of yacht, which he has named *Privacy*.

Achievements and Successes

Tiger's dream to be a professional golfer came true early in his career. In only his first year playing professionaly, Tiger earned $940,420. Since then, he has gone on to have many successes and achievements. To date, he has earned more than $80 million in tournament prizes.

Tiger has been named Player of the Year nine times and Male Athlete of the Year four times by the Associated Press. He has also been honored in the California Hall of Fame.

Tiger has won a great deal of prize money, but he earns even more by making commercials and advertisements. Companies pay athletes to wear their clothes, drive their cars, or use their mobile phones. The image of athletes using these products is appealing to many people.

■ In 2008, Tiger won the Arnold Palmer Invitational tournament.

In his first year as a professional golfer, Tiger signed six contracts worth millions of dollars to promote products. In 2000, he signed a deal with the company Nike that was worth more than $100 million. This was the most money any company had ever paid an athlete to promote products. Tiger also works closely with some companies on special projects. He helped Tag Heuer create the first watch designed for golfers.

According to a study by *Golf Digest* magazine, it is believed that Tiger will have earned more than one billion dollars by the year 2010. This will make him the first athlete to accomplish this goal.

THE TIGER WOODS FOUNDATION

In 1996, Tiger and his father started the Tiger Woods Foundation to help kids reach their full potential. In the first 10 years, they helped 10,000,000 children. Tiger then built a 35,000 square foot (3,252 square meter) learning center that allows kids to explore careers. The learning center gives fun courses on more than 50 careers ranging from rocket science to business. All of the courses were designed by kids for kids.

www.tigerwoodsfoundation.org

Write a Biography

A person's life story can be the subject of a book. This kind of book is called a biography. Biographies describe the lives of remarkable people, such as those who have achieved great success or have done important things to help others. These people may be alive today, or they may have lived many years ago. Reading a biography can help you learn more about a remarkable person.

At school, you might be asked to write a biography. First, decide who you want to write about. You can choose a golfer, such as Tiger Woods, or any other person you find interesting. Then, find out if your library has any books about this person. Learn as much as you can about him or her. Write down the key events in this person's life. What was this person's childhood like? What has he or she accomplished? What are his or her goals? What makes this person special or unusual?

A concept web is a useful research tool. Read the questions in the following concept web. Answer the questions in your notebook. Your answers will help you write your biography review.

- What did you learn from the books you read in your research?
- Would you suggest these books to others?
- Was anything missing from these books?

- Where does this individual currently reside?
- Does he or she have a family?

- Where and when was this person born?
- Describe his or her parents, siblings, and friends.
- Did this person grow up in unusual circumstances?

Your Opinion

Adulthood

Childhood

WRITING A BIOGRAPHY

Main Accomplishments

Help and Obstacles

Work and Preparation

- What is this person's life's work?
- Has he or she received awards or recognition for accomplishments?
- How have this person's accomplishments served others?

- What was this person's education?
- What was his or her work experience?
- How does this person work; what is or was the process he or she uses or used?

- Did this individual have a positive attitude?
- Did he or she receive help from others?
- Did this person have a mentor?
- Did this person face any hardships?
- If so, how were the hardships overcome?

Timeline

YEAR	TIGER WOODS	WORLD EVENTS
1975	Tiger is born on December 30th.	Ruffian, the fastest racehorse in history, dies during the last race of the year. This was the only race she ever lost.
1979	Tiger completes nine holes of golf with the low score of 48. He is three years old.	"Magic" Johnson is signed to the LA Lakers. He becomes the highest paid **rookie** in history, with a $500,000 contract.
1991	Tiger becomes the youngest golfer to win the U.S. Junior Amateur Championship.	Mike Powell beats the longest standing Olympic world record for the long jump. To this day, no one has beaten his record.
1996	Tiger becomes a professional golfer at the age of 21. This same year, he creates the Tiger Woods Foundation.	Softball is introduced as an Olympic sport. The US women's team wins the gold medal.
2000	Tiger is the youngest PGA golfer to get a "grand slam," winning all four major tournaments in one year.	Anthony Ervin sets the record for the 50-meter swim. His record of 21.21 seconds is still unbroken.
2004	Tiger marries Elin Nordegren.	Smarty Jones wins the Kentucky Derby.
2006	Tiger's father, Earl, dies from cancer on May 3rd.	Zinedine Zidane, one of the world's best soccer players, retires.
2007	On June 18th Tiger becomes a father. He and his wife, Elin, name their child Sam Alexis.	The Philadelphia Phillies baseball team becomes the first to lose 10,000 games.
2009	Tiger's second child, Charlie Axel, is born.	Matt Kenseth wins the Daytona 500.

Further Research

How can I find out more about Tiger Woods?

Most libraries have computers that connect to a database that contains information on books and articles about different subjects. You can input a key word and find material on the person, place, or thing you want to learn more about. The computer will provide you with a list of books in the library that contain information on the subject you searched for. Non-fiction books are arranged numerically, using their call number. Fiction books are organized alphabetically by the author's last name.

Websites

Visit Tiger's official website at www.tigerwoods.com

To learn more about golf, visit www.golf.com/golf

Words to Know

aggressive: intense and energetic

cancer: a serious disease which sometimes causes death

comedy: a type of entertainment that uses humor

descent: a family history specific to one area of the world

dimples: small indents on a surface, like craters on the Moon

prodigy: someone who shows great abilities with little training or at a very young age

professional: to make a living at something

rights: basic freedoms of all people, protected by the government

role model: someone we admire and learn from

rookie: athletes in their first year of playing

tournament: a large sports contest between many players

Index